10.56

Successful Mentoring

In A Week

P9-DGV-232

Steven Carter and Gareth Lewis

3M

The Teach Yourself series has been trusted around the world for over 60 years. This series of 'In A Week' business books is designed to help people at all levels and around the world to further their careers. Learn in a week what the experts learn in a lifetime.

Steven Carter is an international management and organization development consultant and CEO of Apter International. His special area of expertise is the development of senior managers, directors and teams.

Gareth Lewis has over 25 years' experience as a consultant in the field of organizational and leadership development. He has worked with a large range of organizations, including many household names, developing HR strategy and systems, and dealing with the management of change.

Successful Mentoring

Steven Carter
and Gareth Lewis

www.inaweek.co.uk

Teach Yourself®

IN A WEEK

Hodder Education

338 Euston Road, London NW1 3BH

Hodder Education is an Hachette UK company

First published in UK 1994 by Hodder Education

This edition published 2012

Copyright © 1994, 2012 Steven Carter and Gareth Lewis

The moral rights of the authors have been asserted

Database right Hodder Education (makers)

The *Teach Yourself* name is a registered trademark of Hachette UK.

British Library Cataloguing in Publication Data: a catalogue record for this title is available from the British Library.

10 9 8 7 6 5 4 3 2

The publisher has used its best endeavours to ensure that any website addresses referred to in this book are correct and active at the time of going to press. However, the publisher and the author have no responsibility for the websites and can make no guarantee that a site will remain live or that the content will remain relevant, decent or appropriate.

The publisher has made every effort to mark as such all words which it believes to be trademarks. The publisher should also like to make it clear that the presence of a word in the book, whether marked or unmarked, in no way affects its legal status as a trademark.

Every reasonable effort has been made by the publisher to trace the copyright holders of material in this book. Any errors or omissions should be notified in writing to the publisher, who will endeavour to rectify the situation for any reprints and future editions.

Hachette UK's policy is to use papers that are natural, renewable and recyclable products and made from wood grown in sustainable forests. The logging and manufacturing processes are expected to conform to the environmental regulations of the country of origin.

www.hoddereducation.co.uk

Typeset by Cenveo Publisher Services

Printed and bound by CPI Group (UK) Ltd, Croydon, CR0 4YY

Also available in ebook

Contents

Introduction 2

Sunday 4
What is mentoring?

Monday 16
What makes a successful mentor?

Tuesday 30
The organization base

Wednesday 42
The development base

Thursday 58
The interpersonal base

Friday 74
The context base

Saturday 88
Implementing mentoring schemes

Surviving in tough times 102
Answers 106
Further sources of information 107

Introduction

If you ask somebody if they have ever had a mentor, and they say 'no', put the same question to them again but slightly differently. This time ask if they have ever had a coach, sponsor or confidant, or a colleague or friend to whom they would always turn for advice or support. If they now answer 'yes', then they have benefited from mentoring but probably never realized it before.

What is a mentor?

In a working environment – the focus of this book – a mentor is someone who will first help you to identify your professional goals, then advise you how to build on your strengths and rectify your weaknesses, with the ultimate aim of bringing out your full potential. This process is usually carried out through a series of regular face-to-face meetings, although mentoring can also be conducted via phone, email or text.

Mentors are – typically but not always – older and more senior than their learners, who are also referred to as mentees, protégés or, in more traditional circles, apprentices. Mentors use their knowledge, experience and skills to steer an individual through a structured learning and development programme that has a clear objective. This could be a qualification or the acquisition of a skill, or something more intangible such as a change in attitude or behaviour.

What are the benefits of mentoring?

Mentoring benefits everyone. The learner can improve their capabilities and confidence, boosting their career prospects and putting them on course to achieving their lifelong ambitions. For the mentor, the process offers the reward of guiding someone to attain their goals, while also supporting their own personal self-development by enhancing their management and leadership skills.

The employer is a winner, too. Specific benefits for an organization include a better-motivated workforce, increased productivity, more effective training and reduced staff turnover. A mentoring programme can also enable an organization to introduce a more open and supportive working culture.

Who uses mentoring?

Despite what you might think, it isn't just large companies that can benefit from, and afford, mentoring programmes. The process is suitable and cost-effective for organizations of all sizes – from micro-businesses to multinationals – and at any stage in their development, whether they are start-ups or have been established for more than a hundred years!

How can this guide help me?

This book is an excellent place to start for someone who has no previous experience of mentoring but who wishes to learn more about the subject. We will provide you with a step-by-step guide which uses jargon-free language, tackling the subject in a general manner that will be appropriate to many different development contexts.

We will answer all your key questions – for example: What makes a good mentor? How do you monitor a learner's progress? What resources will be needed?

The text includes useful checklists and case studies, along with easy-to-understand descriptions of the practical measures you will need to take to establish and manage a mentoring programme successfully. All this in just seven days... so let's get to work!

SUNDAY

What is mentoring?

We will begin our week-long learning journey by giving some thought to the concept of mentoring. Many of you will be familiar with the word but perhaps not fully understand what it means. It might strike you as being a completely modern idea because of the increasing use of mentoring schemes by organizations over the last couple of decades. In fact, it's a term that has been around for thousands of years.

Neither is the application of mentoring confined to the business world. It is common in many spheres of life, such as sport and the arts, to name just two. Consider your own experience: you may have had a mentor or been a mentor yourself – but never realized it at the time! So you might know a lot more about mentoring than you think.

Mentoring can offer many other benefits apart from the learner's personal development. The mentor gains, too – the process can improve their working relationships with colleagues and assist their own self-development. Then there are obvious benefits to the organization through having more productive, more capable and more motivated employees.

In the final section of this chapter, we will learn how mentoring schemes are similar to other management processes in that goals need to be clearly defined at the outset, resources allocated and progress monitored.

SUNDAY
MONDAY
TUESDAY
WEDNESDAY
THURSDAY
FRIDAY
SATURDAY

An new phenomenon?

In recent years, the idea of mentoring has appeared in the management development lexicon. You could therefore be forgiven for thinking that it was a new idea. However, like most good ideas, it has been around for a long time. In fact, the term comes from the Greek myth in which Odysseus, departing for the Trojan War, leaves his son Telemachus under the tutelage of his old friend Mentor.

In the modern era, you might frequently come across the term in many areas of human activity, from sports through to the arts, as well as in management.

Think about these examples:

- the old boxer who takes a young boxer under his wing, trains him and advises him while his career progresses
- the manager who recruits a new employee and spends time with them showing them the ropes about the organization and the job
- the manager who has been trained to support and advise an employee a Chartered Management Institute certification programme
- the team leader of a sales team to whom all the others go when they have problems.

These examples differ in terms of how systematic they are, and in their levels of formality. However, they are all examples of mentoring in action.

If you think about your personal experience at work, you will probably also realize that you have either had a mentor (or more than one), or have been a mentor. This is important because it tells us two things. First, most of us already know a lot about mentoring (even if we didn't know the term). Second, it illustrates that mentoring is an effective and natural component of good management.

So what is mentoring in a development context? We can describe it as:

> a process where one person offers help, guidance, advice and support to facilitate the learning or development of another person.

It usually involves some of the following characteristics:

- the mentor is older
- the mentor is more experienced
- the mentor is more senior
- the mentor has knowledge and skills to pass on.

It is worth emphasizing that mentoring is not an additional management task. Its main function is to enhance performance and to support people in their natural development.

It is clear from these examples that a great deal of mentoring has gone on over the years, although it may not always have been called mentoring, and may not even have been recognized as such.

Similarly, we would contend that good managers have always been good mentors. What has changed more recently is that management commentators and educators have recognized the benefits and have tried to approach and use the concept more systematically. So much so that mentoring is now used in a planned way in many contexts.

Some examples include:

- induction training
- career progression
- managing projects
- mutual mentoring in change situations
- formal learning programmes.

The benefits of mentoring

This passing on of knowledge and understanding, 'showing people the ropes', has many benefits. These benefits can be gained if the mentoring happens as a natural and informal aspect of the management process, or if it is part of a more structured and systematic development programme. We can look at these potential benefits from three points of view:

1 the mentee (we shall call them learners)
2 the mentor
3 the organization.

Clearly, the learner has much to gain from such a relationship, although exactly what they gain will depend on the skill of the mentor and the nature of the programme.

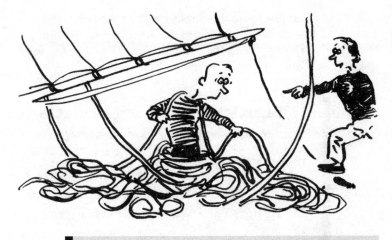

SUNDAY

MONDAY

TUESDAY

WEDNESDAY

THURSDAY

FRIDAY

SATURDAY

Benefits to the learner

Mentoring enables the learner to:
- get to know the culture and political ropes of an organization
- develop skills
- receive feedback on performance
- gain access to resources
- find increased clarity and definition of goals.

It would be easy to think of mentoring as a 'give' relationship, but our experience has shown that the process also offers benefits to the mentor.

Benefits to the mentor

Mentoring:
- assists in management tasks such as monitoring performance, communication, etc.
- increases satisfaction and reward in the job
- increases motivation and performance of mentored staff
- assists personal self-development.

Anything that enhances good relationships among staff is bound to have benefit for the organization involved. However, there are some further, specific benefits for organizations in structured mentoring programmes.

> ## Benefits for the organization
>
> For an organization, the existence of a mentoring scheme can bring about:
>
> - improved succession planning
> - more effective management development
> - faster induction of new employees
> - improved communications
> - reduced training costs
> - reduced turnover of staff
> - increased productivity.

The process of mentoring

Clearly, many of these benefits can result from both **formal** and **informal** mentoring. However, we intend in this book to concentrate on planned and systematic programmes.

Mentoring programmes, or programmes with a mentoring component, are very much like any other management process:

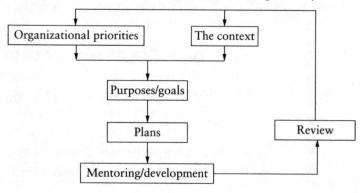

This external loop looks at the whole process from the point of view of the organization.

Purposes or goals

As with any other project, the purposes of the programme need to be defined. Not only do they need to be stated, but they need to be agreed and communicated.

Within the totality of the programme (which will relate to the goals of the organization), there needs to be a statement of the purpose of the mentoring component of the programme. If there is a lack of clarity here, there is a possibility of conflict between the mentoring relationship (the needs of the individual) and the greater goals of the project (the needs of the organization). This will be dealt with in more detail in further sections.

Plans

Again, the outcomes and achievements from the programme need specifying and relating to a time frame. The principles are the same as those for any other project.

Resourcing

Resourcing in this context refers specifically to the selection and training of the mentors. This training needs to cover both the nature of the programme itself and the skills of mentoring.

SUNDAY

MONDAY

TUESDAY

WEDNESDAY

THURSDAY

FRIDAY

SATURDAY

Mentoring

This is the internal loop that defines the nature of the mentoring relationship itself:

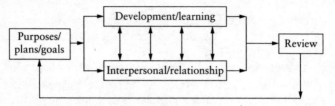

The process has two major aspects:

1 developmental/learning
2 interpersonal/relationship.

These form two of the four bases of mentoring that are covered later in the week.

Summary

So what have we learned about mentoring on our first day? Well, we know a little more about the origins of the term and that it has been around a lot longer than many people realize. While mentoring is being increasingly used by organizations, it has long been commonplace in areas of human activity that have nothing to do with the world of work.

We have also seen that structured mentoring programmes can be used in various situations – induction training, career progression, and so on – to aid the personal development of the learner. What's more, there are specific benefits for the mentor and the organization.

Perhaps the most important point to remember from this chapter is that a mentoring programme, to be fully effective, must be treated like any other management process. Time and thought must be devoted to planning, scheduling and resourcing. The desired outcomes must be defined, agreed and communicated. There should be regular reviews to assess the progress made towards meeting these objectives. This is why we say that a good manager is a good mentor, and a good mentor is a good manager.

Tomorrow we will go on to look at what makes a successful mentor.

SUNDAY

MONDAY

TUESDAY

WEDNESDAY

THURSDAY

FRIDAY

SATURDAY

Fact-check (answers at the back)

1. What is the origin of the term 'mentor'?
   a) Freudian psychoanalysis theory ☐
   b) 21st-century management speak ☐
   c) Roman folklore ☐
   d) Greek mythology ☐

2. Which of these are examples of mentoring in action?
   a) An old boxer training a young boxer ☐
   b) A manager showing the ropes to a new employee ☐
   c) A team leader guiding junior staff ☐
   d) Telling somebody how to make the tea just the way you like it ☐

3. Complete the following sentence: 'Mentoring is an effective and natural component of good _____?'
   a) Matchmaking ☐
   b) Meditation ☐
   c) Manipulation ☐
   d) Management ☐

4. What are typical characteristics of a mentor?
   a) More experienced ☐
   b) More senior ☐
   c) False teeth and grey hair ☐
   d) Has knowledge and skills to pass on ☐

5. Complete the following sentence: 'Mentoring's main function is to enhance performance and to support people in their natural _____?'
   a) Habitat ☐
   b) Environment ☐
   c) Development ☐
   d) World ☐

6. Which of these are contexts where mentoring can be used in a planned way?
   a) Induction training ☐
   b) Career progression ☐
   c) Half-time in a football match ☐
   d) Formal learning programmes ☐

7. What are some of the benefits that the learner can gain from mentoring?
   a) Skills development ☐
   b) Feedback on performance ☐
   c) Access to resources ☐
   d) Free sweets at meetings ☐

8. What are some of the benefits that the mentor can gain from mentoring?
   a) The chance to shout at people ☐
   b) Job satisfaction ☐
   c) Motivated staff ☐
   d) Personal self-development ☐

9. What are some of the benefits that the organization can gain from mentoring?
a) Faster induction ❏
b) Reduced training costs ❏
c) Reduced turnover ❏
d) Increased productivity ❏

10. Complete the following sentence: 'As with any other project, the purposes of the [mentoring] programme need to be _____?'
a) Imagined ❏
b) Ignored ❏
c) Forgotten ❏
d) Defined ❏

MONDAY

What makes a successful mentor?

If you've got the Monday morning blues, today's thoughtful discussion will ease you into the working week. Having looked at some of the things that mentors might do for an individual or organization, we will now look at how mentors might achieve these things.

First, we will examine how mentors can ensure they fully understand the expectations of learners. To do this, mentors should imagine they are in the learner's shoes and then ask themselves a series of questions:

- What does the learner need?
- What does the learner want to achieve?
- What are the learner's motivations?

Next, we will consider some of the tasks that mentors will have to perform in order to support an individual's learning and development. The role, as we will see, involves more than passing on expertise and experience – a key added responsibility is the provision of social and emotional support.

So can anybody be a mentor? There are skills and qualities that are necessary to be successful in this role. Aside from technical knowledge, you will need interpersonal skills like, for example, being a good listener. Mentors need to be role models, too, and we will give you some examples of positive and negative ones.

Expectations of learners

A useful way of describing the sorts of things a mentor needs to do to help a learner is to look at the situation through the eyes of the learner. What does the learner need?

A mentor is supporting the development of an individual and will need to consider:

● the particular motivation and goals of the learner
● the commitment and resources of their organization to help an individual meet those goals
● the skills of the learner.

A key criterion for successful mentoring must be the ability of a mentor to respond to these three factors in a positive and useful way.

A mentor, therefore, needs to be able to understand what is motivating an individual to learn in the first place. Of course, there are many different factors in the motivation to learn and mentors should try and understand the particular goals of whomever they are trying to mentor. There are, however, some commonalities. These might include:

● problems to deal with
● career progression
● increased job satisfaction

- personal development
- increased performance
- achieving organization goals.

The last of these common goals raises an interesting point. Who is setting the learner's goals? If they are set by the organization, then a mentor needs very quickly to understand what an individual's motivation is towards achieving these goals. One-hundred-per-cent commitment is an easy but often erroneous assumption to make.

Successful mentoring needs resourcing. Resources include time, materials and work, and mentors can take a vital role in securing these, particularly when an organization has not adequately thought through its responsibilities in developing staff.

A mentor needs to be able to support a learner in regard to the particular strengths and weaknesses a learner has in the process of development. Whatever the specific functional or technical skills, a learner will probably need to employ some of the following:

- learning skills
- setting goals
- identifying their own learning needs
- planning their own learning

- listening
- accepting help and feedback
- taking risks.

So what do mentors do?

We said that mentors facilitate and support the learning and development of others. But how do they do this?

This will differ from person to person and will depend, to some extent, on the purpose and nature of the context in which it takes place. However, the following list is a good description of the general tasks involved in the process arising from the learner needs outlined above.

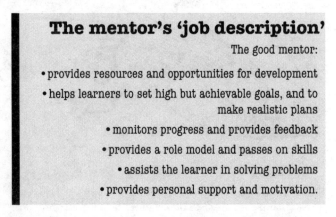

The mentor's 'job description'

The good mentor:

- provides resources and opportunities for development
- helps learners to set high but achievable goals, and to make realistic plans
- monitors progress and provides feedback
- provides a role model and passes on skills
- assists the learner in solving problems
- provides personal support and motivation.

In undertaking these tasks, successful mentors will be doing so in a way that does not just 'go through the motions'.

Nearly all learners, whatever development they are undertaking, will at some time find it daunting and possibly stressful. As important as the technical expertise and knowledge that they bring to a mentoring relationship, mentors therefore also need to provide social and emotional support. Often it is this aspect of a mentor's behaviour that will determine the success or otherwise of the mentoring relationship.

Who can be a mentor?

This is quite an ambitious list and you might wonder who these paragons of virtue are that are able to perform all of these tasks. One answer to that question is to think again of your own personal experience, and of those people who have helped and supported you at some time in your professional life. Having done so, it is likely that you will soon be able to point to a positive role model. It is also possible that you may think of a few negative role models that show you exactly how *not* to do it!

But it is true that good mentors do have certain skills and qualities that predispose them to be good mentors. Later in the week we will propose a model of the whole process that will enable us to define the skills required. Today, we want to suggest a set of qualities that you should look for in selecting mentors, or seek to develop in yourself.

Mentor qualities

Undoubtedly, one of the key qualities a mentor must have is relevant **work experience**. It is not that mentors need to be a theoretical expert in a particular field, nor as we shall see, is their role centrally one of being a tutor. But mentors will need an understanding, which may be partly intuitive, of what a learner is trying to achieve.

Related to this is that mentors also ideally need **experience or knowledge of the organization** in which the mentoring relationship takes place. Furthermore, they need to understand through this experience 'how things get done around here' and be able to mobilize organizational support and opportunities to help a learner's development.

Mentors, of course, need excellent **interpersonal skills**. They need to be good at asking questions, they need to be good listeners, they need to appear supportive and flexible in their approach and need to come across as people genuinely interested in the development of others.

Finally, mentors should be **good role models**. They should be credible to a learner, demonstrating an open approach, accessibility and many of the key behaviours that a learner may be trying to develop (such as personal organization, management style, etc.).

The list above can be used for the purposes of self-assessment. Use the following form to rate yourself (or get others to rate you) on a 1 to 5 rising scale against each of the qualities. This might give you some ideas about your own development needs as a potential mentor.

	1	2	3	4	5
Work experience	L	I	I	I	J
Organization experience	L	I	I	I	J
Relevant interpersonal skills	L	I	I	I	J
Role model	L	I	I	I	J

You should keep these in mind as you read through the rest of this book, which will discuss these issues in much more detail, hopefully giving you the information you need to develop yourself as a mentor.

Role models

Perhaps one of the best ways to discover how to mentor is to consider the people who have helped you learn and develop through your career. Consider for a moment what it was about them that was particularly useful. What made the difference for you? What did they do well, what was it they said, did, arranged that was important to you in your career development? Without over-analysing their attitudes and behaviour, a very good way of starting to enhance your skills as a mentor is simply to copy their approach. The insights and understanding will come later as you experience the role of helping others develop for yourself.

Alternatively, you could consider someone whose career has flourished despite their inattention to the ideas of good practice that we have set out. Thinking of their attitudes and behaviour will give you help in understanding what might be expected of a mentor, by doing the opposite to them.

Do any of these fairy godmothers and wicked uncles ring any bells?

Fairy godmothers

- **'Managementors'** do two things well. First, they have the personal skills to manage the process itself. This involves time management and the ability to plan, set goals and action plans, and deliver objectives. Second, they have knowledge, skills and experience of the substantive areas of learning.
- **'Agreementors'** have the ability to give responsibility at the right time and in the right way. They have the skills to delegate and negotiate to a high degree. They are therefore also **'Empowermentors'** with a flair for appropriately releasing responsibility.
- **'Developmentors'** believe both in self-development and the development of others. They intuitively seem to know what people need to understand and learn and this is demonstrated by their words and deeds. Developmentors will have a track record of involvement in the learning and development of themselves and others.

- **'Experimenters'** are tolerant of ambiguity, are happy to try things out for themselves and encourage others to do the same. They often question the status quo and never assume that they – or anyone else – has all the answers. They understand that learning is about making mistakes and can accept failure if it results from the right motives and intent.
- **'Implementors'** get things done. They can transform thoughts and ideas into action. They know where to find the resources required, and the information and support that will make the difference. Implementors tend to be pragmatic, action-oriented, and are usually good problem-solvers. They are often close relatives of the **'Achievementor'**, who sets and delivers high but achievable goals, and expects others to do the same.
- **'Assessmentors'** can provide feedback that is clear, open and unbiased. They are critical in an objective way, i.e. not afraid to report what they see whether it is positive or negative. They do this in a way that avoids blame, personal comments, judgements but, instead, focuses on the future. Their honesty is accepted because they build up trust, demonstrating interest and care for others and offering any comments with appropriate timing.

Wicked uncles

- **'Argumentors'** involve themselves at a subjective level. They can appear to be 'interviewing' in conversation, seeking to influence, interpret and ascribe hidden motives. They are unable to tolerate different points of view and seek to bring others, through challenge, around to their point of view. They are closely related to the **'Judgementor'** who is inflexible, critical and always right. They should try agreeing and listening (*see* **Agreementor**).

- Far too directive, **'Regimentors'** never let people try things out for themselves or do things in a different way. They only ever see one way of doing things – their way! They have a strong tendency to impose goals, timetables, solutions and opinions. They should try flexibility and empowering behaviour (*see* **Developmentor** and **Empowermentor**).

- **'Cementors'** have a tendency to get people stuck – and leave them to dry! They hate change and regard organizational structures as something designed to fix people into roles. Changing roles and responsibilities upsets them. They firmly believe that people should know their place. They often say – when confronted with a new idea – that they've seen it all before. They should try commitment, flexibility, problem-solving (*see* **Managementor** and **Experimentor**).

● The biggest failing for **'Commentors'** is that they talk too much. They have an opinion on everything. They also have a tendency to think that they are right, and can easily drop into playing the expert. What they are not good at is listening. They should try listening and giving responsibility (*see* **Agreementor and Developmentor**).

Summary

After today, you should have a better idea of the range of tasks a mentor is expected to carry out. One of the most important is to discover what is motivating an individual to learn and what they hope to achieve. Often the answers to these vital questions can be found by looking at things from the perspective of the learner.

The other duties expected of a mentor will depend, to a large extent, on the individual needs of the learner and the context in which their learning takes place. We should not forget that some learners might be overawed by the demands of their development programme. This is where the support of a mentor can be critical.

You should also be familiar with the essential skills and qualities that you should look for if you are charged with selecting a mentor, or the ones you should aspire to learn and develop if you want to be a mentor yourself. One way to learn how to mentor is to emulate the positive role models you have encountered in your own career – and do the opposite of any negative ones you might know!

SUNDAY

MONDAY

TUESDAY

WEDNESDAY

THURSDAY

FRIDAY

SATURDAY

Fact-check (answers at the back)

1. What are the key factors a mentor should consider when assessing the needs of the learner?
   a) Motivation and goals of the learner ☐
   b) Whether they take milk in their coffee ☐
   c) Commitment and resources of employer ☐
   d) Skills of the learner ☐

2. What are some of the common goals that might motivate a learner?
   a) Career progression ☐
   b) Increased job satisfaction ☐
   c) Personal development ☐
   d) Passing an audition for *Britain's Got Talent* ☐

3. What are some of the behaviours that will be expected of a learner during the mentoring process?
   a) Listening ☐
   b) Making paperclip chains ☐
   c) Accepting help and feedback ☐
   d) Taking risks ☐

4. What are some of the tasks that a mentor will be expected to carry out during the mentoring process?
   a) Provide resources ☐
   b) Help the learner to set goals ☐
   c) Monitor progress ☐
   d) Judge who's made the longest paperclip chain ☐

5. Again, what are some further tasks that a mentor will be expected to carry out during the mentoring process?
   a) Help the learner to make realistic plans ☐
   b) Pass on skills ☐
   c) Assist the learner in solving problems ☐
   d) Provide personal support ☐

6. What aspect of a mentor's behaviour will often determine the success or otherwise of the mentoring relationship?
   a) Buying drinks down the pub ☐
   b) Taking the learner out for a romantic dinner ☐
   c) Providing financial support ☐
   d) Providing social and emotional support ☐

7. What are some of the essential skills and qualities of a good mentor?
   a) Relevant work experience ☐
   b) Experience or knowledge of the organization ☐
   c) Being a whizz at crosswords ☐
   d) Interpersonal skills ☐

8. What are the attributes of a good role model?
   a) Good looks ☐
   b) Credibility ☐
   c) Open approach ☐
   d) Accessibility ☐

9. Which of the following is not an example of a 'fairy godmother' type of mentor?
a) Managementor ☐
b) Agreementor ☐
c) Terminator ☐
d) Implementor ☐

10. Which of the following is not an example of a 'wicked uncle' type of mentor?
a) Argumentor ☐
b) Cementor ☐
c) Commentator ☐
d) Commentor ☐

TUESDAY

The organization base

Having explored the background we can now go on to look in more detail at the tasks and processes involved in mentoring. We will do this by introducing you to a model that describes the four dimensions or bases of competence involved in mentoring.

These describe a sequence and areas of activity, as well as a means for measuring strengths and weaknesses of mentors, schemes and participating organizations.

We will analyse all four bases – see diagram below – in turn over the next four days. To start things off, in this chapter we will give you a brief description of each one before focusing on the organizational base.

We will then go on to examine the two major dimensions of the organizational base: organizational readiness and positional strength.

With the former dimension, we learn how systems, culture and management style can determine if a mentoring scheme succeeds or not, while, during our discussion on the latter dimension, we consider the importance of the mentor's position within the organization and how this can have a bearing on the credibility and, hence, the success of a scheme.

The four bases of mentoring

Let's look in more detail at the tasks and processes involved in mentoring. We will do this by proposing a model that describes the four dimensions or bases of competence involved in mentoring. They describe a sequence and areas of activity, as well as a means for measuring strengths and weaknesses of mentors, schemes and participating organizations.

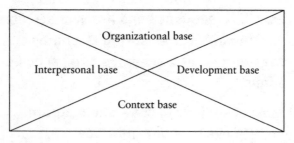

We will analyse each of these bases in turn over the next four days, beginning today with the organizational base. Before we do that, however, we should give a brief description of each.

The organizational base

This base relates to the positional strength of the individual mentor (or team of mentors) within the organization, and to the readiness or 'fit' of the process to the culture of the organization. Mentoring is much less likely to succeed if it does not have legitimacy and support from the organization as a whole, and particularly from senior management. The positional strength of mentors shows commitment, but also puts into the system a substantial core of expertise, experience and knowledge of the organization.

The organizational base is related to the qualities of management perspective, organizational know-how and credibility.

Interpersonal or relationship base

Any structured relationship requires commitment and skills to understand and empathize with the needs of others. In many ways, this is the core area of skill, because without it the rest will not follow. It is related to the qualities of accessibility and communication.

The developmental or learning base

Most contexts in which mentoring is featured have learning or development as a component. It is therefore important that mentors have some understanding about the notion of learning, particularly about learning at work.

This base is related to the qualities of developmental orientation and flexibility.

The context base

This base involves the purposes of the developmental relationship. The requirements will change depending on whether the context is formal or informal, whether it is a structured programme of learning, and so on. It also has a limiting or defining effect on the other three bases.

We will now go on to study each of these bases in more detail.

The organizational base

The organizational base of mentoring has two major dimensions. These are:

1 organizational readiness
2 positional strength.

In this base, we focus on the need for the process in the organization, on the culture and power structures within which it will take place, and on the ability of the mentors to implement or deliver the scheme. In fact, the second and third of these facets are very closely related, but are here set out first from the perspective of the organization as a whole, then from that of the individual mentors.

Organizational readiness

We can describe the differences between organizations in a number of ways. Even organizations which are involved in the same business can go about it in quite different ways. Those differences can be described in a number of ways. The kinds of distinction that are often used include:

- different structures and methods of organization
- different styles of management
- different cultures
- different systems
- different ways of making decisions – both formal and informal.

Consider these two theoretical examples:

A civil service department

It is hierarchical and bureaucratic. People in positions of authority are usually there for their professional or technical expertise rather than management competence. People are expected to do what they are told. Mistakes are framed as failure, and are not tolerated. There is a correct way to do everything, and innovation is not sought. Change is considered as a threat.

A young software company

This company is quite small (80 employees) and has an atmosphere more like a club. There is no rigid or hierarchical management structure as the staff work in teams. It works on a project-by-project basis in teams, and the opinions and contributions of all staff are invited and valued. It lives and works in a fast-paced and innovative environment. Co-operation is seen as the key to the company's success.

The question that we shall be interested in is whether these two different companies can *both* support successful mentoring schemes. The answer, of course, is that it *is* possible. However, experience tells us that one of them is much more likely to be suited to support the learning and development of its staff at work.

An *individual, informal* mentoring relationship can thrive and be successful in almost any environment, but is easier and more likely to succeed in the right environment. Systematic mentoring schemes, however, can only succeed where the right conditions prevail.

It is not simply a matter of saying that mentoring will not work with certain styles of management. However, it is precisely these kinds of influences that affect the success of mentoring within an organization.

Some of the factors that are known to be conducive to the notion of mentoring are included in the checklist below:

✔ a supportive culture
✔ unintentional failure is tolerated
✔ job roles are flexible
✔ staff are respected and consulted
✔ staff are given authority to make decisions
✔ open communication is encouraged
✔ there is high concern for people.

It is worth giving due consideration to these factors when thinking about the appropriateness of a potential mentoring scheme within an organization. Realistically, though, there are many organizations that do not correspond to the above profile in every detail. Equally, there are organizations where mentoring is seen as a part of the way to changing the environment.

In these cases mentoring can succeed, but two further elements need to be strongly in place:

1 **Visible top management support** This is necessary for two reasons. First, it is a declaration of intention and importance. Top management support communicates a powerful message about the need for change, and the ways in which it can be achieved. Second, a scheme supported by the senior management is likely to receive the practical resourcing necessary to make such a scheme a success.

2 **Developmental bias** There needs to be a shared understanding that only by developing people can an organization change and improve performance. Added to this, there needs to be an appreciation that real learning can take place at work, as well as in the classroom or training room.

In other words, there needs to be shared recognition, not that learning is important, but of *how* it can happen.

For this reason the success of many schemes can be attributed to the efforts of a 'champion' who can communicate

with, and persuade, senior management about the benefits of
the style of learning implicit in many mentoring schemes.

Positional strength

This leads us on to consideration of the position of the
individual mentor within the organization. This positional
strength of the mentor is important because of the credibility
of the scheme, which will affect its chances of success.

It is also important because positional strength will
influence access to available resources. Mentoring efforts can
founder for lack of resources – particularly time and training.

The following checklist provides a set of indicators about the
optimum conditions for successful mentoring.

Positional strength	1	2	3	4	5
Access to information					
Access to informal network of alliances					
Perspective on organization					
Access to decision-making processes					
Commitment from the powers that be					
Credibility of the individual					
Influence of the individual					

Summary

Today we have looked briefly at the four bases of mentoring, and then went on to examine the organizational base in detail. To recap, this base relates to the readiness of an organization to introduce mentoring.

It is possible for organizations of all kinds to operate informal mentoring schemes successfully. But the chances of success will be higher in those organizations where certain conditions exist – for example, a supportive culture, open communication and a flexible management structure.

If where you work does not fit the ideal profile for a mentoring organization, do not despair! A scheme could still succeed if:

- it has the overt backing of the top management, *and*

- there is a wide understanding that the organization will only grow and develop if it helps its people to grow and develop.

We also talked about the positional strength of the mentor, which has important implications for a mentoring scheme with regard to its credibility and access to resources.

SUNDAY
MONDAY
TUESDAY
WEDNESDAY
THURSDAY
FRIDAY
SATURDAY

Fact-check (answers at the back)

1. Which of these is not one of the four bases of mentoring?
   a) Organizational base ☐
   b) Interpersonal base ☐
   c) First base ☐
   d) Development base ☐

2. Complete the following sentence: 'Mentoring is much less likely to succeed if it does not have legitimacy and support from the organization as a whole, and particularly from senior _____?'
   a) Citizens ☐
   b) Railcard users ☐
   c) Management ☐
   d) Moments ☐

3. What are the qualities related to the organizational base of mentoring?
   a) Management perspective ☐
   b) Being neat and tidy ☐
   c) Organizational know-how ☐
   d) Credibility ☐

4. What are the qualities related to the interpersonal (or relationship) base of mentoring?
   a) Accessibility ☐
   b) Anonymity ☐
   c) Condescension ☐
   d) Communication ☐

5. What are the qualities related to the developmental (or learning) base of mentoring?
   a) Orienteering skills ☐
   b) Developmental orientation ☐
   c) Inflexibility ☐
   d) Flexibility ☐

6. What are the two main dimensions of the organizational base of mentoring?
   a) Organizational readiness ☐
   b) Mental strength ☐
   c) Physical strength ☐
   d) Positional strength ☐

7. Which of these factors are known to be conducive to the notion of mentoring?
   a) A supportive culture ☐
   b) Dress-down Fridays ☐
   c) Flexible job roles ☐
   d) Staff respected and consulted ☐

8. Again, which of these factors are known to be conducive to the notion of mentoring?
   a) Free biscuits in the office ☐
   b) Staff are given decision-making authority ☐
   c) Open communication ☐
   d) High concern for people ☐

9. Complete the following sentence: 'There needs to be a shared understanding that only by _____ people can an organization change and improve performance.

a) Sacking ❏
b) Demoting ❏
c) Demotivating ❏
d) Developing ❏

10. Which of these are indicators of the positional strength of a mentor within an organization?

a) Access to information ❏
b) Access to informal network of alliances ❏
c) Access to the stationery cupboard ❏
d) Access to decision-making processes ❏

WEDNESDAY

The development base

The development base of mentoring covers just about everything to do with learning. It is consequently a key area of competence for would-be mentors, as most situations in which mentoring takes place at work involve learning and development in one form or another.

In our working lives we have constantly to adjust and develop. The emergence of new economies, growing competition and advances in technology means we should not just accept change, but proactively embrace it. Individuals who fail to learn new skills could find they become prime candidates for redundancy if their old skills are no longer needed. Organizations that fail to evolve and innovate, bringing forth new products and services, will simply stagnate and eventually die.

So learning and development should be an intrinsic part of modern working life, for individuals as well as for organizations. In a true learning organization, learning and productive activities are looked up on as being one and the same.

Today, then, we will consider:

- why learning is important
- how people learn at work
- the learning cycle
- different styles of learning
- learning to learn.

Mentors are not teachers

Before we begin to examine why learning is so central to the business of mentoring, we should make an important distinction. Many people confuse the role of mentor with that of 'teacher' or 'tutor'. The roles are quite different. The focus of the roles of both teacher and tutor is the imparting of knowledge. Both roles are appropriate to school-based or academic education.

Mentoring is a much broader role than this, with a much wider focus. Although knowledge can be important, and coaching has a place in mentoring, it is not necessary for a mentor to be an expert on all topics.

We shall explore these distinctions more thoroughly later on.

Why learning is important

In terms of learning at work, there are three factors that influence us and require that we learn and develop:

1 **Work itself is changing** As markets, competitive forces and technology change, these put pressure on organizations to change. This in turn puts pressure on us to develop new ways of working. Change and development are wired in to

most jobs, and these will involve us in continually learning new skills.

2 **Career progression** Most of us have a need to progress within our jobs. For most of us this takes the form of the acquisition of responsibility and seniority. The days when we held the same job for life are gone. As well as progression within a role or organization, we often seek progression between jobs and organizations. Job mobility is now part of our way of professional life.

It is implicit in both of these factors that we develop and learn as we go along.

3 **Personal satisfaction** Human beings have natural curiosity and need for variation. So we seek out opportunity, and this also involves a learning process.

However, in order for us to be able to learn, certain conditions need to be satisfied. These include:

- **environmental conditions** such as resources, opportunity and support
- **personal conditions** such as motivation, commitment and the ability to learn.

In order to understand how we, as mentors, can influence these, we need to look in more detail at how people go about learning at work.

Learning at work

For many of us, our attitudes to learning are framed by our experience of school and formal education. This version of learning usually involves a process that goes something like this:

1 There is a 'teacher' who is an expert, and knows everything.
↓

2 The 'teacher' tells us what we need to know, and/or how to do what we should be able to know/do.
↓

3 We then get it right and receive a pat on the head, or get it wrong and feel inadequate.

This version of events has a number of important characteristics:

- It is highly dependent on the 'teacher', rather than the learner.
- It concentrates on the acquisition of knowledge.
- It is a hit-or-miss affair where 'failure' is regular and frowned upon.

Of course, we don't want to suggest that all school, or even academic, education takes the form of this description – just that it is many people's *perception* of learning.

The type of learning that we wish to concentrate on is different because adults are different to children, and because learning at work is different to formal or academic education.

We can summarize some of these differences:

Child learning

- Dependent on teacher
- Unrelated to experience
- Subject oriented
- Responsibility for learning rests with teacher

Adult learning

- Independent of tutor
- Relates to experience
- Responsibility rests with learner
- Work oriented
- Failure is tolerated

It should be clear from this that it is not appropriate for mentors to adopt the traditional role of a teacher. In the approach to adult learning implicit in the description above, the responsibility for the learning rests firmly with the learner.

So what role, then, does the mentor take? The answer is that a mentor can help learning in three basic ways. We can categorize these different roles as:

1 facilitator
2 coach
3 learning consultant.

1 The facilitator

The facilitator is someone who provides support and resources to the learner. One of the greatest resources, of course, is time. This might be the time that the mentor contributes, but also important is the time that the learner devotes to the process – not just in talking about things, but also in engaging in or trying out new activities, skills and so on. The fact that mentors are usually more experienced and senior, and have greater influence within the organization, helps enormously in this aspect of the role.

2 The coach

The coach is someone who is able to pass on skill or who is able to monitor and provide feedback to the learner as they attempt to develop skills or new behaviours. This will be dealt with more fully tomorrow.

3 The learning consultant

The learning consultant is one who advises and helps the learner explicitly in the activity of learning. Encouragement and motivation are important here because an adult learner might initially lack confidence in their own learning ability. It is why we have to accept or tolerate a level of failure. In fact, we shouldn't see it as failure, but as an unsuccessful trial from which we can learn.

In order for us to be successful as learning consultants, we should look in more detail at the process of learning as it applies to adults at work.

The learning cycle

A psychologist, David Kolb, has described learning as a circular process. This cycle of learning has four stages, each of which is necessary for learning to take place:

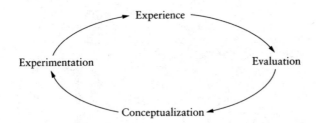

Experience

Work (and life) provide us with plenty of raw material for learning. This often comes in the form of things that go wrong. We all have the experience of sometimes ignoring these things, and therefore not learning from them.

Experience can also be more structured – such as that gained on training courses.

Evaluation

By the use of observation and reflection we can then begin to make sense of our experience. We can begin to notice what happens, and in what circumstances. At this stage we may not yet know the rules of the game, but we are able to detect sequences of events that link together.

Conceptualization

This is the analysis stage. It is where we frame answers to the question 'Why does that happen?' We are able to construct theories and systems of explanations as to why the world behaves in the way it does.

Experimentation

In this phase we test or try out new behaviours based on the system of concepts we have built. Feedback will enable us to judge whether they are successful or not. Even if they are not, we still have some new experience, which returns us to another loop of the cycle.

This 'trial and error' description of learning is a natural process. It can tell us, as mentors, a number of things. First, by questioning behaviour, habits and assumptions, we can stimulate people to move through these phases of the learning process. Second, learning is a complex thing, and we need to give people the opportunity, or space to travel the journey in their own way. It helps to explain why just telling someone how to do something does not always work easily.

Learning styles

All learners will have different needs, strengths and weaknesses in relation to the phases of the learning cycle. These differences give rise to different approaches to learning, or learning styles.

We can explain some of these differences by people's tendency to operate more often or comfortably in different phases of the cycle.

Operating more strongly in one of the phases can be described as a particular style. So there are four basic styles of learning:

1 **Activists** embrace immediate experience. They like the rush of adrenalin and will often take the lead in visible activities such as meetings and presentations.
2 **Reflectors** like to take their time and think carefully before acting. They tend to be cautious and measured in their approach.

3 **Theorists** are comfortable in the world of logic and ideas. They like to have a model or picture of a whole process or situation. They will find it difficult to do something if they do not know its purpose, or how it 'fits in'.
4 **Pragmatists** are the practical ones. They tend not to value theoretical knowledge too highly. When confronted with an idea or a plan they will ask 'But will it work?'

It is important to say that we all operate in all four phases of the cycle: nobody is only an activist, for instance. Most of us have a repertoire of behaviours that we can use in the appropriate circumstances. Equally, however, many of us have tendencies to learn consistently in one of these styles. Do you recognize yourself or people you know in these descriptions?

> We should point out that people can adjust and develop their style, by trying out new and unfamiliar behaviours.

How does all this help us as mentors? If we recognize that someone fits strongly into one of these styles, what do we do? One option is to respect that and tailor learning activities that will suit that style. The other option is to encourage them to do something unfamiliar, or even uncomfortable.

The best response is to do both. In the early stages we will gain rapport and trust by recognizing and respecting people's preferred way of learning. However, once the learner has built confidence in themselves as a learner, one of the great contributions we can make is to help them to try something new.

One of the great satisfactions of mentoring is to see the highly reflective 'shrinking violet' come out of their shell and confidently give a presentation. We can encourage the activist who wades in at the deep end (and often drowns) to step back and think before acting, and to make judgements about the practicality and viability of their options.

TIP *You can read more about the concept of learning styles in P. Honey and N. Mumford's* **The Learning Styles Helper's Guide** *(Coventry: Peter Honey Publications Ltd, revised edn, 2006).*

Learning to learn

Some people are more efficient and experienced at learning. For many adults at work, it may have been a long time since they have engaged actively in learning. Such 'naive' learners may lack confidence in the early stages of a programme, and may need patience and support until they gain more confidence. 'Mature' learners, on the other hand, will have confidence and will be more self-sufficient in relation to their learning.

How can a mentor make a judgement about how 'mature' their learner is? Experience tells us that there are a number of key indicators:

● the capacity to set high but achievable goals
● the level of responsibility they take for their own learning

- previous experience in the subject to be learned
- previous educational experience.

On the basis of these factors, we should be able to make a judgement about a learner's ability to learn. It is worth doing this because the level of learner maturity does influence the way that we mentor them.

The main difference in the way we would mentor learners at different ends of the scale is found in the level of **direction:**

- **Naive learners** may need a higher level of direction – particularly early on in a programme. They are likely to perceive a higher level of direction as being quite appropriate. Of course, it should also be a part of your agenda to help them to increase their level of learning efficiency. This can be done by paying attention to the first two of the factors in the list above. In these circumstances, success breeds success.
- **Mature and efficient learners** will need less direction. By definition, they are used to setting high but achievable goals. They are more likely to perceive a high level of direction as inappropriate or as interfering.

Summary

Today we have seen why learning at work is so important: we need to develop new skills as the organizations we work for adapt to changing market conditions. On a personal level, we also want to further our own careers and achieve job satisfaction.

Then we examined how learning at work is fundamentally different compared to formal education. These differences mean that, rather than being teachers in the conventional sense, mentors have to fulfil other roles to support, advise and monitor the learner.

Next we introduced you to the theory of the learning cycle, and how individuals tend to favour one learning style over another. This is an important consideration for mentors in two respects: first, a mentoring programme should take account of an individual's preferred way of learning; second, a mentor should be prepared to take a learner out of their comfort zone in order to raise their level of achievement.

Lastly, we looked at how some people may have to 'learn how to learn'. Here, we gave you some tips on how to gauge an individual's ability to learn and their level of maturity.

SUNDAY
MONDAY
TUESDAY
WEDNESDAY
THURSDAY
FRIDAY
SATURDAY

Fact-check (answers at the back)

1. What are the three important factors that require we learn and develop in the workplace?
   a) The changing nature of work itself ❏
   b) Fear of missing out on a jolly ❏
   c) Career progression ❏
   d) Personal satisfaction ❏

2. What are the environmental conditions that have to be met in order for us to learn?
   a) Resources ❏
   b) Opportunity ❏
   c) Comfy chairs ❏
   d) Support ❏

3. What are the personal conditions that have to be met in order for us to learn?
   a) Manicured nails ❏
   b) Motivation ❏
   c) Commitment ❏
   d) Ability to learn ❏

4. How is learning at work different to formal or academic education?
   a) It is not dependent on the teacher ❏
   b) It relates to experience ❏
   c) Responsibility for learning rests with the learner ❏
   d) Failure is tolerated ❏

5. What are the three basic roles a mentor can fulfil to support a learner?
   a) Facilitator ❏
   b) Coach ❏
   c) Beauty consultant ❏
   d) Learning consultant ❏

6. Who described learning as a circular process?
   a) David Beckham ❏
   b) David Attenborough ❏
   c) David Kolb ❏
   d) David Cameron ❏

7. Which of these is *not* one of the four stages of the learning cycle?
   a) Experience ❏
   b) Evaluation ❏
   c) Expression ❏
   d) Experimentation ❏

8. Which of these are basic styles of learning?
   a) The activist ❏
   b) The reflector ❏
   c) The theorist ❏
   d) The pragmatist ❏

9. In how many phases of the learning cycle do people generally operate?
   a) One ❏
   b) Two ❏
   c) Three ❏
   d) All four ❏

10. Which of the following are good indicators of a learner's level of maturity?
    a) The capacity to set high but achievable goals ❏
    b) The level of responsibility they take for their own learning ❏
    c) Previous experience in the subject to be learned ❏
    d) Previous educational experience ❏

THURSDAY

The interpersonal base

Today we will look in more detail at the key to successful mentoring: the nature and quality of the working relationship between the mentor and the learner.

We shall first consider the core conditions that have to be satisfied for a positive and beneficial relationship. These require mentors to be equipped with a range of interpersonal skills – notably, being able to understand and accept (without judgement) another person's point of view. Openness and genuineness are other desirable character traits.

Mentors may also have to adopt two distinct roles: counsellor and coach. A **counsellor** is someone who gives guidance on problems of a personal nature, while a **coach** is someone who assists in the attainment of a professional skill. In considering an approach for both roles, you will see that there is a high degree of commonality among the skills and qualities required.

One of the recurring themes of this week is the **empowerment** of the individual learner. This prompts two pertinent questions:

1 At what stage should a mentor intervene in the learning process?

2 How do you help people to make their own decisions?

In the final section, we provide you with some useful advice on helping learners to learn for themselves.

Core conditions

There are certain factors, or core conditions, that are necessary for a mentoring relationship at work to be successful.

Mentoring relationships, particularly where they arise naturally, go beyond normal professional working relationships. They engage both the mentor and the learner in a deeper and more personal way, and their focus is not merely on the task in hand. Research has shown that positive and beneficial relationships such as these tend to satisfy certain conditions, and these imply a certain orientation from the mentor.

There are three core conditions:

1 rapport
2 positive regard
3 congruence.

Rapport is the state achieved when some person (like a mentor) is able to 'lock in' to the information being provided by the other person. It involves noticing and recognizing verbal and non-verbal information. At the conscious level, it also involves being able to understand and appreciate the other person's point of view.

This state is perfectly natural for us, and occurs in all of our most intimate relationships.

Positive regard is being able to accept, without judgement or interpretation, the other person, their point of view, opinions, personality, and so on. It is being able to take them 'for what they are'.

Congruence is characterized by openness, spontaneity and genuineness. It occurs when there is a consistency between our words and our behaviour.

Added to these more general concepts are specific behaviours or skills that are necessary for the maintenance of the relationship:

- maintenance tasks/features
- accessibility
- giving feedback
- appropriate questioning technique
- communication skills
- knowledge of learner.

Two of these deserve some attention in detail.

Giving feedback

We need to be constructive and positive as well as honest in the way that we give feedback. The feedback cycle is crucial to the development of the individual. For some people, it is easy to be harsh or overcritical – in other words, to play the expert. For others, it is easy to be nice without ever giving positive criticism. It is this **positive criticism** that can often be the most helpful.

Keep it positive

When giving feedback, you should focus on:

- behaviour not the person
- observations rather than inferences or guesses
- description rather than judgement
- the specific rather than the general
- factors under the control of the learner.

YES, YES... THAT'S FINE

Knowledge of the individual

It is worthwhile remembering that, whether at the outset or during the course of any relationship, there are a great many pieces of information that we learn, or are offered, about an individual that will inform the relationship. Among these are:

● motivation
● experience
● personal goals
● approach or personality
● learning style and maturity.

It obviously makes sense to adjust our approach to the individual to take account of these factors. They do not entail a set of rules, nor are they prescriptive, but they should make us sensitive to the needs and style of operation of our learners.

It is difficult to summarize or provide a single message from our consideration of the core conditions that surround a mentor–learner relationship. However, running through them all is a theme of **empowering people**. That is, the object is to help people to make their own decisions and to learn in a way that is comfortable for them, while providing resources which enable them to use the opportunities available to them to their maximum benefit.

Counselling and coaching

The two key roles which a mentor can adopt are those of counsellor and coach. Traditionally, the **coach** is seen as someone who assists in the development of a skill or technique, while the **counsellor** is seen as a solver of personal problems.

We would like to question this dichotomy. Coaching and counselling exist at either ends of a continuum which has the process or task at one end, and the individual at the other. At both ends of this continuum there can be problems, and both are framed by skill and goals.

Coaching   Counselling
←――――――――――――――――――――――――――――――――→
Technique/skill   Personal

At either end of the scale, the focus might be different, and the skills of the mentor must shift according to the priorities. We will set out here an approach to both of these roles, but we should emphasize that the repertoire of skills and qualities required for both have a large amount of overlap.

Counselling

The more person-centred type of intervention requires a knowledge of the basic counselling process.

Counselling can be thought of as a three-stage process:

1 information/understanding
2 solutions
3 action.

1 Information/understanding

This is where rapport is established between the two people. The aim will be for the learner to arrive at a cogent definition of the problem, and for the mentor to arrive at an understanding of it.

The key skill here is that of **active listening**. That is, listening which gives the agenda to the talker. Questions should be open, i.e. should not entail a yes/no answer. Understanding should be checked. Interpretation should be minimized.

2 Solutions

At this stage there are two broad aims. The first one is for the learner to achieve a redefinition of the problem.

The process of going through Stage 1 often leads people to a new view of a situation, or new insights. At this stage, they are ready to invent options and to define outcomes, or to set goals. We have already said that both creativity and flexibility are important at this stage. Creativity is required in helping to develop options, and flexibility in respecting options that work for the learner, whatever the preference of the mentor.

Up until now, the mentor may have intervened verbally very little – the key contribution being to allow and encourage the learner to talk. But, at this stage, the style of questioning shifts a little. It can become more challenging and probing. The use of 'Why', 'What would happen if...', 'Are you sure...' type of questions becomes appropriate.

3 Action

This phase is really about making plans, implementing and managing solutions that arise from goals set at the previous phase. The skill is in allowing people to develop realistic and appropriate strategies, and in providing resources for those strategies to be implemented.

The formal and systematic approach to counselling set out above has been established through experience and practice over many years. However, it is worth pointing out that, like many interpersonal skills, it is a perfectly natural process practised by good counsellors – whether they think they know about it or not!

Perhaps you have had the experience of a friend phoning you up with a problem of a personal nature. It is a quite common experience that, however little you talk (or think you contribute), they will thank you for clearing up a problem for them. If you think about such an experience in retrospect you might realize how the conversation fell naturally into the stages outlined above.

Coaching

As we have said, coaching is aimed at the development of skills or techniques, and can be thought of as a specific kind of counselling intervention. What sets it apart from the more general type of counselling is that the goals or outcomes are already known, and they are usually behaviourally specific. It is therefore very useful in the development of competence.

The model set out here is adapted from *Coaching for Performance* (2009, 4th edn) by John Whitmore who sees coaching as involving four stages:

1 Set **G**oals for overall application and individual session
2 Setting out the current position, or **R**eality
3 Generating **O**ptions with plans and strategies
4 Decide **W**hat is to be done, by whom, when and how.

Progress through the **GROW** model is enhanced by questioning and feedback, rather than by instruction.

1 Goals

Goals set should be **SMART**. That is, they should be:

- **S**pecific
- **M**easurable
- **A**chievable
- **R**ealistic
- **T**ime related.

We all have goals such as 'I want to be happy', but if they do not correspond to the criteria above, we will be unlikely to achieve them. The two key features of goals in this context are that we should have a way (or test) to confirm when we have achieved them, and they should be set by the learner themselves.

However, we mentioned in the section on learning on Wednesday that a low-maturity learner may need considerable help to define goals, particularly if they relate to an area of operations with which they are unfamiliar.

2 Reality

This stage is really an ecology check. It concerns all of the facts, figures, resources and people surrounding the goals at Stage 1. Let us give an example:

> ## Case study
>
> Suppose a learner has decided that, to improve their interviewing skills, they will conduct an upcoming interview for a member of staff in their department. This may satisfy all of the SMART criteria for a goal. However, the organization might have procedures and practices to follow. The personnel department may expect to conduct the interview. Colleagues may have a vested interest. All of the surrounding factors need to be taken into account when deciding upon a course of action.

3 Options

This corresponds quite closely with Stage 2 of the counselling model (see above). As with counselling, both the generation and selection of options needs a substantial amount of creativity and flexibility from the mentor.

4 What

It is here that specific plans and courses of action are defined. The allocation of responsibilities and resources are agreed by mentor and learner. Again, monitoring and feedback are essential to the successful completion of this stage.

You may have noticed that not only is there a great deal of correspondence between the processes of counselling and coaching, but that there is also synergy between the coaching process and Kolb's model of learning (see Wednesday).

Both counselling and coaching encourage learners to reflect on their experience, identifying and conceptualizing the key issues, in order to develop plans of action with which to test (experiment) against experience.

Levels of intervention

Throughout this book we have emphasized the importance of empowering the learner to make their own decisions and set their own goals, and of assisting them to solve their own problems. We can help to make sense of this by looking at the ways, or more accurately the levels, at which it is possible for a mentor to intervene in the learning process.

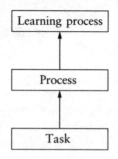

Task

If a learner has a very specific problem, it is possible (and sometimes very tempting) to intervene and solve that problem for them. In acute circumstances it is sometimes necessary to do so. In such situations we are acting as a **consultant** or **expert,** and providing a solution. What we offer in such cases is our specialist knowledge.

Process

Another approach would be to enable the learner to learn or develop the correct solution-finding procedure. In other words, we can teach them the process by which they can solve many similar problems or classes of problem. We would then be a **process consultant**.

What we offer here is the development of skill, and this is more useful than solutions to a specific task because it is more general and more widely applicable.

Learning to learn

At this level, we are a **learning-process manager,** or learning facilitator. Here we encourage people to teach themselves how to find solutions. This is the most general level at which we can intervene. It is therefore the most useful and the most powerful. Not surprisingly, it is also the most difficult.

It is also worth saying that most learners need to gain confidence and 'find their feet' at the lower levels, before they are ready for the abstractness and ambiguity of the higher levels. However, as learners gain that confidence, they become ready for the challenge of learning to learn for themselves.

Self-motivated learning can be considered the end point of a successful and mature mentoring relationship. If your mentoring relationship graduates to this level, you have, by definition mastered all of the ideas set out in this book.

Summary

The relationship or interpersonal base is all about building a relationship between mentor and learner, and then nurturing and managing it. Such relationships are deeper, more personal than traditional working relationships between line managers and the people who work under them.

We saw how feedback is incredibly important, but we need to be careful we get the balance right when giving feedback. If we're reluctant to criticize, the learner will be none the wiser; if we're overly critical, we can damage a learner's confidence. Offering criticism that is honest yet constructive is the best approach.

Today we also learned that mentors can be either counsellors or coaches. Counselling involves establishing a rapport with the learner, identifying their goals or problems, and guiding them towards a solution. Coaching, on the other hand, is more impersonal, and focuses on the development of a particular work-related skill.

Either way, it is important that learners set their own goals and make their own decisions, in other words, they learn to learn for themselves.

SUNDAY
MONDAY
TUESDAY
WEDNESDAY
THURSDAY
FRIDAY
SATURDAY

Fact-check (answers at the back)

1. What are the three core conditions for a successful working relationship between mentor and learner?
   a) Rapport ❑
   b) Positive regard ❑
   c) Congruence ❑
   d) Similar tastes in music ❑

2. Which of these are among the specific behaviours or skills that are necessary for a successful working relationship between mentor and learner?
   a) Accessibility ❑
   b) Appropriate questioning technique ❑
   c) Photocopying skills ❑
   d) Communication skills ❑

3. Which of the following should you focus on when giving feedback?
   a) Observations rather than inferences or guesses ❑
   b) Description rather than judgement ❑
   c) The general rather than the specific ❑
   d) The specific rather than the general ❑

4. What sorts of information about an individual learner should inform the mentor's approach?
   a) Motivation ❑
   b) Favourite TV programme ❑
   c) Experience ❑
   d) Personality ❑

5. The two key roles which a mentor can adopt are those of...?
   a) Good cop and bad cop ❑
   b) Straight man and funny man ❑
   c) Loyalist and rebel ❑
   d) Counsellor and coach ❑

6. Complete the following sentence: 'Coaching and counselling exist at either ends of a _____ which has the process or task at one end, and the individual at the other.'
   a) Conundrum ❑
   b) Conclusion ❑
   c) Continuum ❑
   d) Configuration ❑

7. What can be thought of as the three stages of the counselling process?
   a) Information/understanding ❑
   b) Problems ❑
   c) Solutions ❑
   d) Action ❑

8. Which of these are among the four stages of coaching in the Whitmore model?
   a) Setting goals ❑
   b) Setting out reality ❑
   c) Generating options ❑
   d) Deciding what is to be done ❑

9. What are the three levels at which it is possible for a mentor to intervene in the learning process?

a) Task ☐
b) Recess ☐
c) Process ☐
d) Learning process ☐

10. What can be considered the end point of a successful and mature relationship between learner and mentor?

a) The learner and mentor run out of things to say to each other ☐
b) The learner and mentor both retire ☐
c) The learner learns to learn for himself/herself ☐
d) The learner and mentor get married ☐

FRIDAY

The context base

The context base of mentoring concerns the specific details of the mentoring scheme or individual relationship. Each scheme or relationship will place different demands on both mentor and learner. Today we will outline several broad issues that you as a mentor will have to consider if your relationship is to be successful.

The first of these is the **type of scheme**. Some are informal, with few defined objectives; others are more formal, where a specific outcome is laid down at the very beginning. The latter category includes qualification-based schemes. You will need to adjust your mentoring style according to the demands of the programme.

The **objectives** of the programme will also influence the way you act as mentor. Are the objectives the personal choices of the learner or have they been set by the organization? A further consideration is whether the learner volunteered to be on a mentoring scheme. If not, it might be harder to make the relationship work. This could be equally true where the mentors themselves have been 'conscripted'.

Whatever the context, the responsibilities and expectations of both learner and mentor should be discussed and agreed at the very beginning. We will take you through the terms of reference that, once set out, will help to avoid a mismatch of expectations.

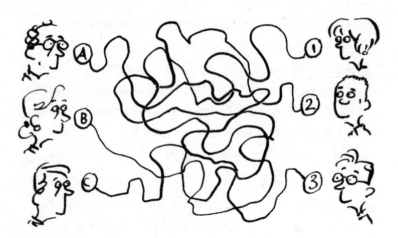

Types of programme

We mentioned on Sunday some of the different types of situation in which mentoring can take place. These included:

- induction of staff
- career progression or development
- learning programmes.

Each of these can differ in the level of formality and the level of their systematization. So within these specific applications there are a number of factors or issues that are worth consideration.

Open-frame mentoring

This style tends to the less formal, with very few specific objectives or deliverables. Usually, the mentor is called upon on the basis of need. It tends to be non-directive mentoring.

Project-based mentoring

This is where there is a specifically defined work-based deliverable or outcome. The mentor will help to define, plan, implement and complete the project in question, and to help the learner to identify and satisfy learning requirements on the way. Some networks of peers operate mutual mentoring on such a project basis.

Qualification-based programmes

More usually found in management development contexts. The programmes may range from in-company provision through to NVQ management programmes or MBAs. They usually involve quite specific learning objectives, rather than business objectives, and a high level of self-assessment. The support offered on non-management programmes tends to be more like that of a tutor than the more complete role of mentor that we have outlined in this book.

> **TIP** *You might like to think how each of these types of approach can affect the mentoring relationship. How do the requirements differ? It might be worthwhile thinking about programmes of which you have experience (or are about to experience), and how they fit into the descriptions given.*

Objectives

Any differences of approach will be reflected in the objectives related to the programme. These objectives will operate at two levels.

1 Objectives carried into the programme

These will be the organizational priorities for the programme in question, and have been discussed in that section. However, it is important that these are visible, shared and agreed upon by both mentor and learner. Where these objectives are quite general, it is part of the role of the mentor to help the learner to translate these into specific and personally relevant objectives, and, if necessary, renegotiate where appropriate.

2 Personal objectives of the learner

These may take the form of statements of outcomes from the programme, or they may be specific learning objectives that arise en route. In general, the objectives of both learner and organization should be compatible. It is important early on in the relationship that a mentor checks out that this is the case, and monitors the situation for any source of potential conflict. Agreement and communication are, of course, essential at this stage.

The objectives of the programme should also help you, as a mentor, to decide what you need to know, and what the learner needs to know. But, as well as the objectives, the processes for managing the scheme should be in place at this stage, along with the resources to implement it. One important resource may be the training of the mentors. On structured programmes this should involve at least a briefing about the details of the programme. It may also involve training of the skills related to the role.

TIP *Processes for managing a scheme should include monitoring and evaluative components. How are mentors going to give feedback to the scheme? How will they communicate with each other?*

All of this information will help you to clarify your role and responsibilities, and to define the limits of your intervention.

Case study

Some years ago the Institute of Management (now the Chartered Management Institute) introduced a mentoring scheme to support the career development of its employees and identified the following objectives:

1 to provide a source of skill and career guidance and support available to all staff

2 to help staff in the development and implementation of their own career development plans

3 to supplement and support activities of managers in developing their staff.

The scheme was entirely voluntary, both for mentors and learners. It was not part of the management process of the Institute or its performance appraisal scheme.

Who mentors whom?

Informal and unstructured mentoring relationships develop on the basis of mutual interest and satisfaction. In more organized schemes or programmes there may be more selection or conscription. Obviously, volunteers and mutual choice are the ideal, but this may not always be possible or practical. Assigned mentor relationships can work very well, although good programmes allow both mentors and learners the right of veto. As a mentor, an important point to check early on is whether your learner is a volunteer or a conscript, as this will affect the relationship.

Of course, there are also many varieties of relationships between these two extremes. An example would be where a pool of mentors is selected and trained, and learners can then select their own mentor from the pool. This increases the likelihood of the relationship working. This is very close to the way the Institute of Management scheme, described above, worked.

One often discussed question is whether a line manager should be a mentor. We believe that mentoring should be a component of any line manager–subordinate relationship. However, for more organized or formal schemes, this is not always the ideal arrangement. Mentor–learner relationships should proceed in an atmosphere of openness and trust. They need to be bounded by confidentiality. They need to be unrelated to issues of promotion, appraisal or salary.

It is possible, therefore, for the mentor relationship and the line manager relationship to suffer from a conflict of interest. It is, therefore, best to avoid this if there is an alternative option. Remember, choosing the alternative option does not reflect on the integrity of any particular line manager. Rather, the learner has much more to gain by widening their perspective through knowledge and experience provided by another objective individual outside the line.

TIP
As mentioned above, training is important – particularly in organized programmes. You should try to define your own needs in respect of this training, in order both to maximize on the training, and to pay attention to your own development throughout the programme.

Terms of reference

Role responsibilities and expectations have already been mentioned. You should be able to articulate these expectations and boundaries, and discuss them with your learner. In this way, there will be no mismatch of expectations – a common cause of the failure of many mentor–learner relationships.

These expectations should be drawn up into terms of reference. If they are not provided by the organization, it can be a useful starting point in developing the way in which you are going to work to draw them up together. They also help to ensure that there is a consistency of purpose and responsibility between you.

The terms of reference should include the following:

- **Confidentiality** Who gets to hear what? Should mentors discuss issues that arise with other people? What are the restrictions?
- **Communication** How do mentors communicate with learners, with each other, with the organization?
- **Timetable** What guidelines are available? How often should mentor and learner meet? Is there a defined end point?

- **Support** If the relationship is not working, what happens? Who mentors and supports mentors?
- **Responsibilities** Are the responsibilities defined for mentor, learner, line manager, scheme sponsor?

The following examples show how the differing circumstances in which mentoring takes place result in specific terms of reference.

Case studies

- A management development officer for **NHS Wales** visited mentors once every three to four months to assess learners progress and monitor the relationships.
- **A large chemical company** set out that mentors should:
  - meet the learner once a month, for an hour, by timetabling formally in advance
  - ensure the learner maintains a brief diary of daily events, to form the basis for monthly discussions
  - develop a personal relationship with the learner
  - maintain the relationship for two years.
- **British Gas** introduced a mentoring scheme to help graduates, who must make frequent job moves within the company during their first few years of development. The aim is to produce a four-way link between mentor, learner, line manager and training department. A key role for the training department is communication. The company published guidelines for the conduct of the relationship, detailing, for example, the time commitment graduates needed to give to the programme, and specific development projects and frequency of meetings (at least once every two months).

> • **AMI Healthcare** introduced a mentoring scheme specifically for senior managers on the company's executive development programme. Mentors were required to support project work which covers an area of work unfamiliar to the learner. Mentors were also expected to have a role in the informal assessment of learners.

These examples may serve to give you some idea of the variety of modes of operation found in mentoring programmes.

Summary

The key lesson from today's discussion can be summed up succinctly: in order to be able to mentor effectively, the context has to be established.

This first thing to consider is the type of mentoring programme being followed and the relevant mentoring style that will be required. Will you be called upon only when needed? Or will you be working closely with the learner at every stage throughout the project? What are the objectives of the programme? These should shape your thinking in respect of how the scheme will be best managed and whether you need to take any action to ensure the right resources are available.

Crucially, too, terms of reference – in effect, ground rules – for the mentoring relationship will need to be drawn up and agreed, making it clear what is expected from both learner and mentor during the developmental process.

We're nearly there – just one more day to go. Tomorrow we conclude by looking at the practical implementation of mentoring schemes.

SUNDAY MONDAY TUESDAY WEDNESDAY THURSDAY FRIDAY SATURDAY

Fact-check (answers at the back)

1. Which of these are among the styles of mentoring that can be applied in learning programmes?
   a) Open-frame mentoring ❑
   b) Long-winded mentoring ❑
   c) Project-based mentoring ❑
   d) Qualification-based mentoring ❑

2. The objectives for a mentoring programme operate at two levels. What are they?
   a) The objectives of the organization ❑
   b) The objectives of the mentor ❑
   c) The objectives of the 'man in the street' ❑
   d) Personal objectives of the learner ❑

3. The organizational priorities for the mentoring programme in question should be:
   a) Visible ❑
   b) Invisible ❑
   c) Shared ❑
   d) Agreed upon by both mentor and learner ❑

4. In general, the objectives of both learner and organization should be...?
   a) Mismatched ❑
   b) Incompatible ❑
   c) Compatible ❑
   d) Irreconcilable ❑

5. Good mentoring schemes allow both mentors and learners to have the right of...?
   a) Entry ❑
   b) Way ❑
   c) Veto ❑
   d) Access ❑

6. Which of these are prerequisites for effective mentor–learner relationships?
   a) Atmosphere of openness and trust ❑
   b) Free snacks ❑
   c) Confidentiality ❑
   d) Unrelated to issues of promotion, appraisal or salary ❑

7. What are the potential drawbacks of your line manager being your mentor?
   a) Conflict of interest ❑
   b) Narrow perspective ❑
   c) Limited exposure to wider knowledge ❑
   d) None ❑

8. What is a common cause of the failure of many mentor–learner relationships?
   a) No expectations ❑
   b) Mismatched expectations ❑
   c) Limited expectations ❑
   d) Great expectations ❑

9. Which of these should be included in the terms of reference for a mentoring programme?
   a) Confidentiality ❑
   b) Office cleaning rota ❑
   c) Timetable ❑
   d) Support ❑

10. In the terms of reference, whose responsibilities should be defined?
   a) The learner's ❑
   b) The mentor's ❑
   c) The line manager's ❑
   d) The scheme sponsor's ❑

Implementing mentoring schemes

Over the last six days we have covered every aspect of the role of mentoring. Our final discussion concerns the practicalities of implementing mentoring schemes.

The first thing to weigh up is the nature of the organization concerned and whether the proven factors that facilitate effective mentoring are in place. We also highlight how a mentoring scheme, just like any other project, needs to be properly planned and managed. This will involve, among other things, monitoring the learner's progress and being able to deal with problems – both unexpected ones and ones you should be prepared for – that may crop up along the way.

In terms of scale, there are of course differences between formal and informal schemes. Generally speaking, the guidance in this chapter may seem to be more relevant to formal learning and development. However, the issues discussed apply to informal situations just as much, even though the need for planning and the organization and commitment of resources is less.

If you have made it this far, and have read through and taken on board the advice provided, you should now be feeling you are ready to be a mentor. What you learn today will help you to put theory into practice.

Factors affecting a scheme

The first consideration with a major scheme which has
a mentoring component is the organization in which the
development activity will take place. If it provides the right
environment and resources, much of the rest can follow
naturally. Introducing a scheme is a major project, and should
be treated as such. The key characteristics of the scheme can
now be considered:

- a supportive work culture/environment
- voluntary participation
- a discriminating selection process
- defined objectives and timeframe
- training and development in content/structure/purposes of
  scheme and personal skills
- terms of reference
- monitoring.

*These factors all help to make a successful scheme. In
planning a scheme, consideration should be given to which
ones are in place, how to put others in place, and how you
can manage without any of the factors.*

There is one other key factor that we have found by experience to be critical. Schemes or major development programmes need a **champion**. In our experience, successful in-company management programmes invariably had a champion role model.

Although we have stressed the need for top management commitment, and that the support of a senior figurehead can add weight, importance and impetus to a programme, this is not what we necessarily think of as a champion. The role of the champion needs more than words, or even visibility. It can be fulfilled in a number of ways.

The first way it can be achieved is by **role modelling** and 'walking the talk'. In other words, we will have a situation where a senior manager or director does some or all of the following:

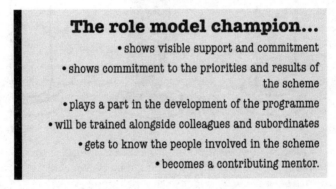

The role model champion...

- shows visible support and commitment
- shows commitment to the priorities and results of the scheme
- plays a part in the development of the programme
- will be trained alongside colleagues and subordinates
- gets to know the people involved in the scheme
- becomes a contributing mentor.

Another version of the champion role is the person (often less senior than the role model champion) who runs the programme or manages the project. They will do many of the following:

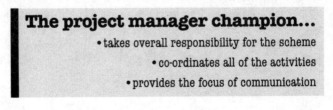

The project manager champion...

- takes overall responsibility for the scheme
- co-ordinates all of the activities
- provides the focus of communication

- becomes the source of information/advice
- becomes the mentor's mentor
- provides the contact with external bodies/suppliers.

The contribution that the project manager champion makes is to 'oil the wheels' and keep all involved on track. In our experience, the success of a scheme can very often be attributed directly to the project manager champion.

Developing a scheme

A development scheme is an activity or project much like any other work-based initiative. So it needs the application of the planning cycle and managing, like any such project.

The planning or managing cycle sets out the steps in carrying out a major task in logical time order:

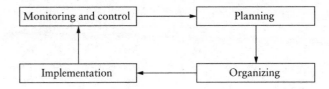

At the planning stage, these are the major considerations:

- objectives
- structure
- resources
- selection
- training
- plans and timeframes.

The detailed consideration of each of these can be found in the appropriate section of this book. There is, however, one resource that is often ignored or underestimated, and that is **time**. It is important to pay attention to the time needed by both mentors and learners in any structured scheme:

- When will the mentoring take place?
- Will meetings/sessions be scheduled or programmed?
- Will it be considered as a legitimate activity in its own right?
- Can 'quality' time be freed up for the required purposes?

It is surprising how often major schemes are planned on the tacit assumption that mentoring is an extra activity, and will somehow just happen on its own. Often it does not.

Implementation

It is always anticipated that projects will roll out according to plan. In a perfect world they always would.

Unfortunately, things do not always work in a perfect way. Much of the skill of delivering or implementing a successful programme comes from adjusting according to events and, in particular, according to needs as they arise. The following ideas might help:

- communication
- support
- performance goals and indicators
- monitoring and on-going evaluation
- communication.

Good lines and mechanisms for communication should be incorporated into any good plan. However, some of the needs will only become apparent in the run time. A good project manager, and a good plan, will make provision for emerging needs. These needs might take different forms. They might include the need for:

- feedback to be shared
- problems to be shared and dealt with
- mentor or learner to network.

Support

The need for good support mechanisms has been emphasized throughout this book. If adequate processes and resources are put into place, then problems can be dealt with without threatening the success of the programme.

Performance goals and indicators

Of course, goals and objectives are important. But global goals need to be translated to the level of the individual learner and the individual mentor. The learner should have clear goals. But how do you, as mentor, know if your intervention is effective or successful? These goals can be framed in terms of performance, in terms of stages reached, in terms of skill or capability, in terms of attitude, or in terms of the relationship.

Indicators or 'signposts' are a way of defining steps along the route to success. It is important for both mentor and learner to lay down some measures prior to the culmination of the process that let you know that things are going well.

Monitoring and evaluation

Having defined indicators, we now have a way of knowing whether we are achieving our goals. This is important in terms of the motivation and satisfaction of the individuals, as well as the success of the whole scheme. Again, processes need to be in place that enable us to evaluate the scheme properly, and to adjust it according to experience. These will need to involve sharing information outside the particular relationship. What provisions are made for this?

Agenda for first meeting

The first meeting is where the style and tone of the relationship is set. From the learner's point of view, it can often involve uncertainty and anxiety. It is important as a mentor to prepare yourself for the first meeting.

So what should happen at a first meeting? Here are some of the issues you might need to discuss:

- life histories/experience
- job roles and responsibilities
- purposes/goals of scheme
- terms of reference/confidentiality
- signposts and targets
- nature of relationship
- times, when and where, how often

- assessment of the learner – their skills, needs, personal goals, etc.
- future meetings...

It is impossible to be prescriptive, but within all of these topics there are two things that carry special importance:

1 The major priority in the first and early meetings is to establish the relationship itself. Gaining rapport, trust and confidence are building platforms for productive and satisfying activity. This is a skill in its own right, and you need to pay conscious attention to it.
2 The other element of the first and earliest meetings is 'meeting discipline'. Some relationships will be naturally low key and open frame. But where there are detailed and specific purposes, and where there is work to do, then there is a message or role model responsibility to lead by example. You should therefore come prepared, agree agendas and keep to time. This is a good skill that you can pass on to the learner.

Problems

Within even the best-planned scheme, it is possible, and even likely, that problems may occur. Good planning, however, should enable you to prevent major, structural problems. The major ones to avoid are:

- **political problems** – where vested interests conflict with the aims of the scheme
- **extra tasks/responsibilities** – where new or arbitrary requirements disrupt the running of the mentoring relationship
- **relationship problems** – such as the assignment of an unsuitable mentor, lack of rapport, or the mentor leaving.

What should be anticipated and dealt with are the minor run-time difficulties that an individual learner might experience on any learning programme. Some of these might be learning difficulties, which can be dealt with by good communication skills and good coaching. Others might be practical difficulties, which may need the experience and expertise of the mentor to solve directly, or to assist the learner to solve.

Some examples to be prepared for are:

- practical problems
- learner too busy
- poor time management
- obstructive line manager
- lack of opportunity/access/information
- competence need – 'I don't know how to...'
- mentor need – 'I don't know either...'.

Winding up a scheme

Most mentoring projects or schemes will have a natural life cycle. This will progress from, possibly, tentative beginnings, through maturity, to end. It should be planned and agreed at the beginning both how and when the relationship will end. It is not good for anyone for important relationships just to cease. The way to avoid this is to discuss and agree a natural endpoint. A proper wind-down and exit should occur, so that both parties can properly readjust to life without the relationship.

Mentoring checklist

Finally, we set out here a comprehensive checklist that will help in the planning and implementing of mentor schemes whatever their scope or nature. The points on the checklist can serve as prompts, either to direct you back into the book, or for further thought or planning.

- Right organization?
- Identified right mentors?
- Scheme evaluation in place?
- Top management commitment?
- Resources?
- Selection and training?
- Matching mentors to learners?
- Terms of reference/guidelines for scheme?
- Contingency plans to deal with problems?
- Support for mentors?

Summary

We've reached the end of our week-long journey. We hope you have found it interesting, informative and inspiring. Let's pause one final time to reflect on what we have learned...

By now you should be familiar with:

- the benefits of mentoring for the learner, the mentor and the organization
- essential qualities and skills a mentor needs
- the four-base model of mentoring
- the ideal working environment for a mentoring scheme to succeed
- how people learn at work and the four basic styles of learning
- the practicalities of implementation.

The aim of this book was not to provide you with all the answers, but to give a firm foundation for further learning. This basic knowledge will stand you in good stead as you take the next steps towards introducing a mentoring scheme to your organization and/or becoming a mentor yourself. Good luck!

Fact-check (answers at the back)

1. Which of these are key issues or areas of activity when setting up a mentoring scheme?
   a) A supportive work culture/environment ❑
   b) Participants are volunteers ❑
   c) Selection is discriminating ❑
   d) Monitoring ❑

2. Complete the following sentence: 'With many in-company mentoring programmes, the successful ones invariably had a role model _____.'
   a) Negative ❑
   b) Celebrity ❑
   c) Famous ❑
   d) Champion ❑

3. What does a role model champion do?
   a) Shows visible support ❑
   b) Shows commitment to the scheme's priorities ❑
   c) Plays a wide range of sports to a high standard ❑
   d) Plays a part in the scheme's development ❑

4. What does a project manager champion do?
   a) Takes overall responsibility for the scheme ❑
   b) Goes AWOL whenever needed ❑
   c) Co-ordinates all of the activities ❑
   d) Becomes the mentor's mentor ❑

5. Which of these are steps in the managing cycle of a scheme?
   a) Planning ❑
   b) Organizing ❑
   c) Implementation ❑
   d) Monitoring and control ❑

6. What issues need to be considered in relation to the timetabling of a mentoring scheme?
   a) Will meetings be scheduled or programmed? ❑
   b) Should learner and mentor synchronize watches? ❑
   c) Will it be considered as a legitimate activity in its own right? ❑
   d) Can 'quality' time be freed up for the required purposes? ❑

7. What can goals or indicators measure or evaluate to help you monitor the learner's progress?
   a) Performance ❑
   b) Skills acquired ❑
   c) Attitude ❑
   d) The number of bad hair days ❑

8. What are some of the key issues that should be discussed at the first meeting between learner and mentor?
   a) Life histories/experience ❑
   b) Job roles and responsibilities ❑
   c) Last night's telly ❑
   d) Nature of relationship ❑

9. What are some of the practical problems a mentor should be prepared for?
a) Learner is too busy ❏
b) Learner's poor time management ❏
c) A wardrobe malfunction ❏
d) Obstructive line manager ❏

10. Complete the following sentence: 'It should be planned and agreed at the beginning both how and when the relationship will _____.'
a) Be announced to the public ❏
b) Be celebrated with a launch party ❏
c) Be featured on daytime television ❏
d) End ❏

Surviving in tough times

In a difficult economic climate, the proven benefits of mentoring schemes can be even more valuable. We've compiled a list of ten top tips – made up of key points worth repeating along with some fresh ideas for you to think about – to help you make the most of what mentoring has to offer when times are hard.

1 Use mentoring to stay competitive

It's a tough old world and competition is increasing all the time. As a result, organizations – of all sizes and in all sectors – have to be able to adapt to changing market conditions and meet demands for innovative products and services. This also means that established jobs have to change and organizations need to teach their people new skills that meet the requirements for newly created roles and functions. Mentoring schemes can make a significant contribution to the success of in-house training programmes by monitoring progress and encouraging individuals to attain their learning goals.

2 Don't forget: mentoring is a money-saver

Do you remember all of the ways mentoring can save you money? For a start, it will enable you to speed up the induction process of new employees, which means they become productive more quickly. Mentoring can also reduce training costs by increasing the percentage of individuals who meet their learning objectives at the first time of asking.

Improved communications in the workplace will result in fewer costly mistakes being made. In addition, development programmes are known to increase the motivation of employees and engender loyalty, which will lead to reduced staff turnover and, in turn, lower your organization's overall recruitment costs.

3 It will help you to keep your best employees

In challenging economic times, it's even more important to keep hold of your most creative, talented and hardworking people. Keeping these key personnel on board could make the difference between survival and failure. We all want to progress in our careers – gain promotion, increase our earning power, broaden our experience, learn new skills and be happy at work. Use tailor-made mentoring schemes to develop your top people and they will be more likely to feel they have a long-term future with your organization and less likely to start getting itchy feet. Think of the money you'll save by not having to pay headhunters to replace your best brains!

4 Harness your workforce's potential

With recruitment freezes affecting many organizations in both the public and private sectors, mentoring will help you to get the best out of the people you've already got. You might be surprised by how much they can achieve with the right support and encouragement. Many bright minds failed to shine at school because they simply weren't suited to an environment where learning is formal and regimented and failure is not tolerated. But they blossom at work when they are given responsibility for their own learning, becoming more capable, more productive employees.

5 The right qualifications

Employers in a wide range of business and industry sectors have complained that school curricula and even university degree courses do not equip candidates with the skills and knowledge they need in the modern workplace. Many formal and academic qualifications are dismissed as being irrelevant. Mentors can help to overcome this problem by identifying gaps in learners' skill sets, and then supporting them as they develop the abilities required by studying for more relevant vocational or business qualifications. These can range from NVQs to MBAs.

6 Don't cut mentoring schemes!

During a recession everybody looks to save money by cutting any unnecessary expenditure. Resist any pressures to shelve your mentoring programme as this could be a false economy. In return for a relatively small investment of time and resources, mentoring can deliver significant economic benefits. Any money you think you will save by not investing in the learning and development of your people could be easily outweighed by the cost of falling productivity and poor service levels, leading to customer complaints and lost orders.

7 Mentoring is good for your reputation

Mentoring is a telling indicator that an organization attaches great importance to the development of its human assets, an area often neglected by less enlightened employers. Thus, organizations that adopt mentoring can improve their standing, credibility and corporate image – in the eyes of customers, suppliers, stakeholders and would-be employees – by being seen as modern, professional and promoting learning.

8 Mentoring is suitable for organizations of all sizes

A number of studies have been published that show how small and medium-sized businesses (SMEs) can benefit from mentoring just as much as a large multinational. These surveys reveal SMEs that had taken up this option were more likely to have grown both their turnover and workforce compared to employers who had not, and expected their businesses to continue to grow in the near future. There is also evidence which suggests SMEs that use mentoring to develop their employees are better equipped to see out an economic downturn.

9 Mentoring is ideal for entrepreneurs, too

We all have to start somewhere. Today's one-man band could be tomorrow's multi-million-pound business employing hundreds of people. But owners of start-up businesses will, by definition, be their own boss and, at least to begin with, will have few, if any, staff. So they are obvious candidates for mentoring. A supportive, trusting working relationship with a fellow, experienced entrepreneur will boost their confidence, develop their leadership and management skills, and ultimately lead to improved business performance and growth.

10 Use mentoring to facilitate change

In this book we have discussed some of the conditions that should ideally be in place for mentoring to be successful. These include a supportive culture, flexible working, devolved decision-making powers and open communication. If these are not present, implementing a mentoring scheme can help an organization to change and achieve these goals. This will be dependent on visible and on-going support from the top management about the need for change. It will also require universal acceptance that an organization can only change and improve if its people are equally committed to the same goals.

Answers

Sunday: 1d; 2a, b & c; 3d; 4a, b & d; 5c; 6a, b & d; 7a, b & c; 8b, c & d; 9a, b, c & d; 10d.

Monday: 1a, c & d; 2a, b & c; 3a, c & d; 4a, b & c; 5a, b, c & d; 6d; 7a, b & d; 8b, c & d; 9c; 10c.

Tuesday: 1c; 2c; 3a, c & d; 4a & d; 5b & d; 6a & d; 7a, c & d; 8b, c & d; 9d; 10a, b & d.

Wednesday: 1a, c & d; 2a, b & d; 3b, c & d; 4a, b, c & d; 5a, b & d; 6c; 7c; 8a, b, c & d; 9d; 10a, b, c & d.

Thursday: 1a, b & c; 2a, b & d; 3a, b & d; 4a, c & d; 5d; 6c; 7a, c & d; 8a, b, c & d; 9a, c & d; 10c.

Friday: 1a, c & d; 2a & d; 3a, c & d; 4c; 5c; 6a, c & d; 7a, b & c; 8b; 9a, c & d10a, b, c & d.

Saturday: 1a, b, c & d; 2d; 3a, b & d; 4a, c & d; 5a, b, c & d; 6a, c & d; 7a, b & c; 8a, b & d; 9a, b & d; 10d.

Further sources of information

If you wish to read or find out more about mentoring, the Chartered Management Institute can provide the following:

- comprehensive booklist and literature search (available from the Management Information Centre)
- personal/individual counselling or mentoring
- consultancy on in-company mentoring schemes.

For details of any of these, please contact the Institute by telephoning 01536 204222 or by sending an email to: enquiries@managers.org.uk.

Notes

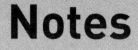

ALSO AVAILABLE IN THE 'IN A WEEK' SERIES

SUCCESSFUL JOB APPLICATIONS • SUCCESSFUL JOB HUNTING • SUCCESSFUL KEY ACCOUNT MANAGEMENT • SUCCESSFUL LEADERSHIP • SUCCESSFUL MARKETING • SUCCESSFUL MARKETING PLANS • SUCCESSFUL MEETINGS • SUCCESSFUL MEMORY TECHNIQUES • SUCCESSFUL MENTORING • SUCCESSFUL NEGOTIATING • SUCCESSFUL NETWORKING • SUCCESSFUL PEOPLE SKILLS • SUCCESSFUL PRESENTING • SUCCESSFUL PROJECT MANAGEMENT • SUCCESSFUL PSYCHOMETRIC TESTING • SUCCESSFUL PUBLIC RELATIONS • SUCCESSFUL RECRUITMENT • SUCCESSFUL SELLING • SUCCESSFUL STRATEGY • SUCCESSFUL TIME MANAGEMENT • TACKLING INTERVIEW QUESTIONS

For information about other titles in the series, please visit www.inaweek.co.uk